GINGERBREAD GEMS
OF OCEAN GROVE, NEW JERSEY

TINA SKINNER
WITH A FOREWORD BY WAYNE T. BELL

Schiffer Publishing Ltd

4880 Lower Valley Road, Atglen, PA 19310 USA

Type set in Zurich BT

ISBN: 0-7643-2394-6
Printed in China

Published by Schiffer Publishing Ltd.
4880 Lower Valley Road
Atglen, PA 19310
Phone: (610) 593-1777; Fax: (610) 593-2002
E-mail: Info@schifferbooks.com

For the largest selection of fine reference books on this and related subjects, please visit our web site at **www.schifferbooks.com**
We are always looking for people to write books on new and related subjects. If you have an idea for a book please contact us at the above address.

This book may be purchased from the publisher.
Include $3.95 for shipping.
Please try your bookstore first.
You may write for a free catalog.

In Europe, Schiffer books are distributed by
Bushwood Books
6 Marksbury Ave.
Kew Gardens
Surrey TW9 4JF England
Phone: 44 (0) 20 8392-8585; Fax: 44 (0) 20 8392-9876
E-mail: info@bushwoodbooks.co.uk
Website: www.bushwoodbooks.co.uk
Free postage in the U.K., Europe; air mail at cost.

Acknowledgments

First of all, this book would not be possible were it not for the homeowners and tenants of Ocean Grove who labor year round to make this place a sparkling gem both of architecture and atmosphere. With them lies the credit of all things beautiful displayed in this book. Moreover, these same people greeted this photographer with hellos and proffers of help instead of the pointed enquiries one might expect while aiming a camera at a stranger's home. Often people came out to share tidbits of history about their homes, and others even invited me in!

Time and again residents recommended that I contact "Ted" Wayne T. Bell, a local historian and author apparently known by all. No sooner did I contact him than I was an invited guest, ushered to a comfortable rocker on his shaded front porch on the north side of town. Mr. Bell took time and care in pouring over the pictures and captions in this book, gently correcting my many little mistakes, and contributing insight that only the town's favorite historian could add. His books, moreover, were invaluable in my research. No lover of Ocean Grove should be without them: *Images of America: Ocean Grove* and *Ocean Grove in Vintage Postcards*.

Finally, special thanks to my publisher, for enabling me to lead a lifestyle that involves strolls along beach community boulevards, business meetings on boardwalks, and opportunities to savor the nation's best architecture.

Foreword

Tina Skinner's first introduction to Ocean Grove involved her driving through the brick and stone gates into a collage of colorful well-kept Victorian homes lining every street. Her first visit evolved into another day trip, into another, and another, finally culminating in a week spent with her Cannon F-4 camera, walking every street to capture pictures of hanging baskets, gingerbread, shaded porches, balustrades, and rooflines.

This National Historic District of Victorian era homes (1870-1910) has been carefully preserved in this book by Schiffer Publishing, Ltd., a company notable for its art-quality production books. Anyone with this book in hand can also enjoy the beauty of Ocean Grove either in their comfortable easy chair at home or on a stroll through the town, as this book serves as an indispensable guide to the diverse architecture of Ocean Grove.

Unfortunately, the author has identified two problems – she wants to take more pictures for another book since there are so many Victorian homes that she couldn't include and, secondly, how can she move beach sand and salt air back to her front lawn in Pennsylvania.

She hopes that you enjoy her selections and that you make plans to visit Ocean Grove to explore this unique town on the Jersey Coast.

Wayne T. Bell
Ocean Grove Historian

Introduction

Ocean Grove is a magical place, almost lost both in geography and time. This tiny 320 acre community lies sandwiched between Asbury Park to the north, the urban beach of rock fame and race riot horror, and Bradley Beach to the south, a typical American beach town almost indistinguishable from the many other seaside resorts stretched along 127 miles of glorious New Jersey coastline.

Ocean Grove, founded in 1869 as a seaside revival camp by Methodists, still offers an otherworldly retreat. With no looming hotels to lure great crowds, and no forty-foot neon carnival attractions to lure board walkers, it has enjoyed a measure of obscurity amidst summer flocks. It remains a place where, in the deepest heat of summer, strollers can still pass along tree-lined avenues in the evening and hear their own footfalls.

The history of Ocean Grove no doubt helped preserve the community when in 1976 it was nominated and placed on the National Register of Historic Places as a unique example of a planned Victorian Community. It has been deemed the largest concentration of Victorian style architecture in the nation. Diligence by the local Historical Society of Ocean Grove, the Ocean Grove Homeowners Association, Township of Neptune, and other groups, plus an overall love of community within the town, have combined to keep "God's Square Mile" just that.

Most Jersey guidebooks have Ocean Grove listed as a must-visit place. The carved and painted decorations that adorn nearly every home in the town are breathtaking in their entirety. More importantly, though, the town offers an opportunity to visit a place evocative of American idylls like the Mayberry of Andy Griffith fame, or Tom Sawyer's stomping ground in small-town Hannibal. In Ocean Grove, one is transported to a seemingly safer, more innocent era, where picket fences and rose privets frame pretty houses, proudly painted in bright, happy hues. People call hello from porch rockers, and retirees lining the boardwalk benches will happily chat about the weather.

At the town's heart, the great Auditorium, a beautiful Victorian tabernacle designed to seat up to 9,000 faithful, sits at the head of a wide, grassy boulevard lined by great architecture and terminating in the Atlantic Ocean. On summer Sunday mornings, church bells toll and the streets fill with the smartly dressed, heading toward the town's pride and joy. In the winter, the services hunker down into a still sizable brick church, St. Paul's on Embury Avenue.

After services, local restaurants tempt with brunches and ice cream cones on a slow-paced Main Avenue, lined with shops every bit as pretty as the homes that surround them.

Whether possessed of the means, or simply possessed by the dream, a visitor soon starts fantasizing about life in Ocean Grove year-round. They feel safe here, comfortable, and welcoming. Small cottages, protected by historic-district codes, inspire a dream of a more simple life. Ocean breezes and shade trees temper even the summer sun's intensity, and children play in the streets under a neighborhood's watchful eye.

As an author and photographer, visiting this town and her citizens has been a privilege; helping to memorialize its beauty a true honor.

At the heart of Ocean Grove stands The Auditorium, a Sunday morning mecca throughout the summer. It was completed in a mere 92 working days (sans work on the Sabbath) and finished in time for camp meeting in the summer of 1894. It towers over the town at 131 feet tall, seats 9,000 earthly souls, and commands the broad vista of Ocean Pathway stretching several blocks to the Atlantic.

The Aurora, 1884, at 5 Surf Avenue. The endless scrollwork provides breathtaking effect.

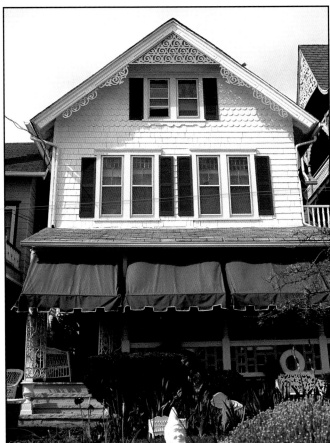

Curvilinear scrollwork underlines the roof at 7 Surf Avenue.

Fish-scale shingles underline the roofline and a conical turret at 7 Surf Avenue.

Painted wood mouldings around arched windows adorn a yellow cottage at 23-1/2 Surf Avenue.

A swoop of roof shelters a generous sweep of second-floor porch.

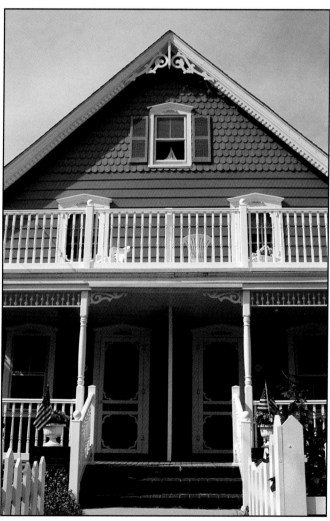

Pink ornaments and shutters are one more layer on this inviting cottage of glazed white gingerbread and green-shingles at 19 Surf Avenue.

Cottages at Bath and Pilgrim's Way mirror the tent architecture they evolved from. Pinnacles and awnings provide adornment.

Besides making guests feel they've entered an enchanted space on the second floor of The Bath Avenue Guest House (7 Bath Avenue). Old-timers hold that a blue ceiling discourages bees from nesting, and thus it was often used on the porch ceilings of Victorian homes.

A charming cottage reflects the creativity of its carpenters, with a baluster of circular cutouts and the elegance of arched doors and windows at 29 Bath Avenue.

Double doors open to a second floor lookout framed in elaborate cutwork at 21 Bath Avenue. A ready and inexpensive supply of white pine boards at the turn of the century, along with the invention of the scroll saw, allowed carpenters the freedom to add elaboration to newly built homes, and for us to enjoy their work today!

The quintessential "wedding cake" house, elaborately frosted in lacey layers of white, stands at 15 Bath Avenue.

Salmon-colored fish scales and white balusters characterize 9 Bath Avenue. A wonderful stained glass window illuminates the interior beside the front door.

A sweet little cottage, caped by a mansard roof, and underlined by a miniature picket fence, stands at 13 Bath Avenue. Blue and white lend it a nautical nature, but it is the profusion of flowers that completes this idyllic scene.

A witch's hat crowns the tower of a cottage at 3 Bath Avenue, with a sailing ship weather vane adding stature.

Neighbors on Ocean Pathway, two homes seem to provide support to each other with rooflines set off-center in popular Victorian style. One yellow, the other light green, they even complement each other in hue.

Boarded up for winter, the eaves at 7 Ocean Pathway are resplendent in gable ornamentation. A collar tie, arched collar brace, and central King post are beams that actually support the roof structure. The rest is mere folly, and all who enjoy the sight are the richer for it.

The three stories of this home were adorned at 9 Ocean Pathway, the heavy ornamentation layered with shades of blue and gold trim. The first-floor balustrade is a unique study in three-dimensional ornament, with cutout windows alongside turned balusters. The Doric portico, too, has been lavished with ornaments.

The Eastlake architectural style was popular between 1870 and 1880. This home at 11 Ocean Pathway is a classic example of that style, with massive, railings and balusters turned on a mechanized lathe, embellished with stylized elements.

A creamsicle home with a conical turret and sunburst windowhead draws stares at 13 Ocean Pathway.

Pink, white, and a spot of purple match the whimsy of carved wooden ornaments that issue from this house at 15 Ocean Pathway.

Ocean Pathway streetscape looking along the North side toward the Atlantic Ocean. The setback requirement created at the town's founding ensures that all property owners for the first two blocks would enjoy sea views and breezes. The planting of view obstructing trees in the first two blocks is also prohibited. These are two reasons why Ocean Grove is a unique Victorian planned community.

A gaily painted cottage at 23 Ocean Pathway with beach colors highlighting rows of fishscale shingle turned columns. Ornamentation on the cornice have likewise been brought to light with paint.

Curved beams add flair to the profile of 29 Ocean Pathway. Saw-tooth cuts on the open stick work attest to the time and attention paid by nineteenth century craftsmen.

Centennial Cottage at McClintock St. and Central Avenue stands as a "showpiece of Ocean Grove's Pioneer Days." The cottage and grounds are maintained by volunteers of the Historical Society of Ocean Grove.

Wide balusters add an aura of privacy to three tiers of balcony at 11 Pitman Avenue.

In some disarray, a cottage at 32 Beach Avenue awaits a summer spruce up. The bead curtains and flower pots attest to the seasonal love adorned on this space.

Cool colors defy the summer sun at 15 Pitman Avenue.

A corner bay adds architectural interest outside and creates a wonderful, octagonal room within.

A streetscape at Pitman and Beach Avenues.

Ocean blue and white, freshly painted and underlined by crisp awnings, invite at 23 Pitman Avenue.

A peach of a home, decked with white woodwork and blue textiles at 25 Pitman Avenue.

Fancy brackets adorn round porch columns on this white cottage at 27 Pitman Avenue. Presumably a bit of gingerbread broke away under the third floor eaves.

Red trim outlines enviable arches at 35 Pitman Avenue.

The Angel sits at Pitman and Central Avenue, in the yard of avid Ocean Grove historian Helen Hurry. The original statue, commemorating the 1778 Battle of Monmouth was destroyed by a coastal storm in the 1930s. This model was created by the Historical Society to raise funds for a new statue.

As though wrapped in lace, this wonder in white graces Ocean Grove at 35 Olin Street. A plaque marks it as one of the city's "Century Homes," having witnessed the life of the town for over 100 years.

Blue and yellow add beach-appropriate accents to the 31 Olin Street address.

While the immediate façade sports a fresh coat of playfully chosen hues, the rest of this building on Olin Street is in the throes of a thorough exterior renovation.

Dated 1886, this handsome yellow cottage at 25 Olin Street is clad in scalloped siding and trimmed in lavender.

A wealth of woodwork was bestowed upon the second-floor façade of this home at 11 Olin Street. Yellow clapboard wraps the front, while shingles shelter the sides.

Brackets decorate the post corners on this cottage at 7-1/2 Olin Street, where porches predominate. The central finial has been anchored by a cross, symbolic of Ocean Grove's origin as a Methodist camp meeting retreat.

Touches of blue have been added to this wonderful yellow cottage at 7 Olin Street, where white scrollwork fills every nook created by support posts on the second floor. A plaque declares this structure one of Ocean Grove's oldest houses, dated 1873. Beside it, the merest of wee cottages sits almost like a garden shed in the side yard. This 10-foot cottage is all original, with the round columns added later.

The carefully restored Majestic guesthouse at 19 Main
Avenue boasts a wonderful slate roof and conical tower.

This pretty cottage at 13 Main Avenue was built around 1895 according to its present owner, who has occupied the house for over sixty years. Originally named The Magic Cottage, it was once a store where souvenirs from the Far East were sold.

Now a dentist's office, this structure at 64 Main Avenue is one of the downtown's more colorful attractions. The bracketed roof is Italianate in style, a school of architecture extremely popular at the turn of the century. With the only sheet-metal façade in town, this building presents floral swags on its bay windows and under the cornices with dramatic results.

Gifts by Tina is a wonderful building, inside and out. Within, dolls, antiques, and other estate and recreated treasures help hark back to the time when this wonderful Queen Ann style structure was built. This is a rare "big" house in Ocean Grove. Its varied roofline is replete with a tower, an onion-domed dormer, and two triangular porticos, plus gingerbread, fish-scale siding, and amazing doors, making this house at 73 Main Avenue is a treasure unto itself.

A wonderful palette of salmon and purple and maroon makes this house at 102 Main Avenue an eye catcher. A colorful addition adds guest accommodations.

An angel flag marks the entrance to 127 Mt. Hermon Way, an eggplant and pink home where the pink curved scrollwork and painted shingles are sure to capture the eye from half a block away.

A yellow cottage at 136 Main Avenue is neatly trimmed in blue and yellow.

Red shingles and white trim stand in pretty contrast at 65 Benson Avenue.

Bright blue with red and yellow trim help this house stand out at 104 Cookman and New Jersey Avenues.

A quaint cottage and shed adorn an expansive garden at 104 Franklin Avenue.

Lacy scrollwork drips from the eaves at 101 New Jersey Avenue.

Painted yellow and white, a contemporary scrollwork artist (circa 1950s) chose to portray flowers and musical notes at 53 Franklin Avenue.

Sweet little summertime cottages line Stockton Avenue.

White gingerbread adorns a shingle-style home at 51 Franklin Avenue. Shingle Style was a particularly popular school of architecture in the late 1800s, at the time most of Ocean Grove's cottages were being built. Traditionally these shingles were not painted, but were allowed to weather.

Little yellow cottage twins sit at 127 and 127-1/2 Broadway.

Fancy medallions adorn a collar under the witch's hat on a second-floor bump-out. These are only a few of the unique features of this colorful house at 106 Broadway, where loving attention has been lavished, evidenced by the carefully applied colors of paint that highlight rows of fishscale shingles.

Flowers add additional ornament to an, airy, open cottage façade with fancifully turned porch posts at 104 Broadway.

A generous swoop of roof caps three tiers of brightly balustered cottage at 92 Broadway.

This cottage at 84 Broadway is arguably the most adorned home in the Grove, every inch of its exterior lavished with Victorian-era bric-a-brac, ironwork, and even lighting. The evidence of an avid gardener spills over the sidewalk and borders the street. Getting shots that revealed the original fish-scale structure was a challenge.

The cottage at 64-1/2 Broadway is a pretty pink and white confection.

Enormous stretches of decking shelter this Victorian beauty on Broadway. The owners, Ann Marie and Denis McCarthy, removed aluminum siding in 2002 to reveal all original woodwork. They've lavished their treasure with yellow, maroon, and green shades.

Arched windows and doors, along with a creamy drapery of bric-a-brac trim, create a lovely image at 58 Broadway.

The Lullaby cottage at 50 Broadway is dated 1879, and sports a
patriotic flare. Such stars and
stripes bunting are com-
mon in the Grove, and
the July 4th parade is
one of her proudest
annual moments.

Creamsicle colors call attention to the fancy woodwork on this Abbott Avenue cottage.

A pretty pink and yellow Queen Anne at 10 Abbott Avenue, complete with a three-story corner turret.

A wonderful conical roof is the center-piece in a mountain range of lines crafted atop 17 Abbott Avenue on the corner of Beach Avenue.

A long expanse of home claims the lot at 14 Abbott Avenue. Beautifully weathered shingles have been decorated with white railings and capped with a green roof.

Unique, drilled details characterize
the balustrades at 21 Abbott Avenue.

An angled shot reveals the substantial mass of post that went into constructing the porch supports on this 1880 Historic Home. The second floor double doors swing out to draw in ocean breezes.

Octagonal turrets with polychrome tiles top this magnificent home gracing the corner of Webb and Central Avenues. Painted shingles, inspired by the slate roof, are the first to catch the eye, and lead one through the fantastic loops and turns created for this fanciful home.

Three houses on Abbott Avenue sport different Victorian finishes. Number 50 is a beautiful, dark shingle style home, iced in white.

Exterior studs imitate Tudor architecture on the eave of this home at 62 Abbott Avenue. Below, interesting geometric bric-a-brac frames the porch, imitating brick-work in its arrangement.

Wonderful corner cutouts have been hung with wooden valances, painted to match lacey orange cutouts that accent the green home at 70 Abbott Avenue.

A blue cottage and garden at 63 Abbott Avenue has been lovingly draped in flowers, and framed with a mini picket fence.

An unusual corner entrance provides access to 107 Abbott Avenue. Fishscale shingles have been carefully painted to lend character to this colorful home.

Cool green and white colors soothe the eye at 74 Abbott Avenue. The Victorians answer to a lack of electric air conditioning was latticework doors. Strips of wood set at an angle ensured the occupants privacy from prying eyes, but allowed the passage of cooling breezes through windows and doorways.

54

A pink and blue palette evokes tropical fantasies at 106 Abbott Avenue.

A wealth of cut-out work on the balustrades and under the eaves belies the fact that this is indeed a small cottage at 77 Delaware Avenue. The owners, however, revel in a wealth of outdoor play space.

A detail shot of 76 Heck Avenue reveals a beautiful color scheme, built up with blue, grey, and white hues.

Hints of color add jeweled facets to this brown house, neatly gardened and surrounded by the idyllic white pickets at 116 Abbott Avenue.

Layers of peach and blue were added to this home at 83 Heck Avenue, like hues in the horizon of a setting sun. The upper roof's front slope, which provides a more rounded appearance to the home, is called a "jerkin head" or "clipped gable".

A conical roof rises above the octagonal, third floor turret of a home on Heck and New York Avenues, adding stature and awe.

This wonderful home at 62 Heck Avenue would be easy to miss for the trees. A detail shot of the balcony reveals the splendor that's obscured.

Pink is a perennial favorite in Victorians, with many a painted lady dubbed "the Pink House." This one at 58 Heck Avenue was a Neptune Township Centennial Home, 1879-1979.

Pink bump-outs add architectural interest to the façade of 56 and 56-1/2 Heck Avenue.

A pretty front porch, framed in bric-a-brac and adorned with mauve and pink painted details, graces the sidewalk at 48 Heck Avenue.

Purple and gold add gaiety
to the balustrade of a home
on Heck Avenue.

A stunning shade of purple
grabs the attention of passerby
at 22 Heck Avenue.

Above:
The Carriage House on Heck Avenue presents a typical Victorian boarding house – with a slate mansard roof happily constructed to create plenty of living space on the third floor.

A wealth of white woodwork trims this stick-style beauty at 16 Heck Avenue.

An octagonal tower creates an addition to the typical two-storey Ocean Grove cottage at 13 Heck Avenue, where lace-trimmed first- and second-floor porches are a predominate feature.

Arched windows and two predominate roof peaks add architectural distinction to 14 Heck Avenue.

Eggplant-colored trim highlights the support posts and draws attention to the elaborate scrollwork that fills every nook at 12 Heck Avenue.

Every architectural additive has been given its day on this yellow home at 8 Olin Street, with a palette of slate green, cream, blue, and eggplant utilized to highlight its many fancywork features.

In a town where porches predominate, a balcony is a welcome architectural respite. Two grace this stately structure at 30 Olin Street, where a palette of slate green, blue, and cream have been applied for nautical effect.

Sans the bric-a-brac, this cottage at 38 Olin Street sports subtle adornments in fish scale shingles and a hint of purple trim.

One of the few fire-resistant buildings in a town of wooden Victorians, the Washington Fire Co. #1 was built of brick on the corner of Olin Street and Central Avenue. It is constructed in typical Italian Villa style, popular between 1830-1880. Also stationed in the building is the E.H. Stokes Fire Co. #3.

A bold, and steady, hand applied blue hues to stripes of shingle at 68 Olin Street.

Grey and pink stripes underline the bracketed room that mark this house at 77 Olin Street as Italian Villa style.

The house at 80 Olin Street presents three wonderful central arches on the second floor, overhung by a roof bedecked in bold gingerbread.

Panels were added in lieu of cutout balustrades, creating privacy for the occupants of this pink cottage at 111 Asbury Avenue.

Extremely detailed work graces the fan brackets and balustrade at 109 Asbury Avenue, prompting a lingering second and third look.

A unique cottage at 107 Olin Street includes a second-floor deck encircled by custom picket fencing complete with little portholes that coordinate with the vergeboard under the eaves.

Paint, a wreath, and a floral awning help add ornament to this colorful home at 104 Mt. Carmel Way thus fits in with it's gingerbread-encrusted neighbors.

Tent city in Ocean Grove. In postcards and photos from around the continent, you can find Victorians making camp in tents just such as this. Even in horse-drawn excursions, they brought such sturdy tents to bivouac among natural wonders such as the Redwoods and Sequoias out West. In this case, such a concentration arrived for the Methodist camp meetings, that a tent city sprung up. The bases and canvas housing for these "temporary" summer-time only homes now stand year round in Ocean Grove. Come late spring, renters busy themselves decorating, adding colored awnings, hanging plants, comfortable bedding, and much more. Within the "campsite" atmosphere, there is great camaraderie, and admirers of the tent porches are likely to be invited to poke their head inside of the tent for a look, as well.

A lavender lady at 92 Mt. Zion Way is blessed with two owners. Their meticulous restoration has encompassed inside and out on this home, including a lavish landscape that extends from the top floors, across a newly installed, heated sidewalk, to a small town park they planted.

Fancy cutouts draw the eyes to
the eaves at 14 Ocean Pathway.

A gambrel roof caps an enormous Victorian guest house, the Ocean Plaza at 18 Ocean Pathway.

The enclosed second-floor porch creates a distinctively different appearance at 18 Ocean Pathway, but no doubt comes in handy during inclement weather, when beachgoers are forced to stay in.

A pretty white on white gothic at 42 Ocean Pathway.

A tented roof caps a pretty pink and green trimmed Queen Anne at 36 Ocean Pathway.

Neutral tones play down this pretty structure. Dental moulding and a pretty collar tie under the eaves are among the fancywork extras.

In keeping with her neighbors, this relatively recent comer to Ocean Pathway incorporates
Victorian-era characteristics, a conical tower, and eye-popping purple and sea green.

A modicum of ornament allows the simple, clean lines of this structure at 12 Ocean Pathway to stand out.

A conical roof and decorative woodwork characterize this corner home at 21 Abbott Avenue. Recent renovations uncovered the decorative woodwork on the gables.

Lots of architectural detail and decorative paint adorn this home at 21 Abbott Avenue. The site is distinguished as a "Century Home" by a plaque.

An extended roofline, termed a "pent," negates the need for an awning to keep the first-floor porch shady at 31 Broadway. A playful palette of green and purple adorns this handsome home.

Yellow with white trim is the pastel perfect picture of the home in a small town at 67 Broadway.

Gingerbread in color and presentation, this handsome shingle-style home graces the street at 69-1/2 Broadway.

Cool peppermint eye candy
for passerby at 87 Broadway.

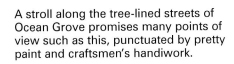

A stroll along the tree-lined streets of
Ocean Grove promises many points of
view such as this, punctuated by pretty
paint and craftsmen's handiwork.

Picturesque in pastels, pretty houses are on parade along every Ocean Grove street. In this case, three pastel princesses line Webb Avenue.

A tiny cottage, two rooms deep, at 27 Seaview Avenue.

A finial and pendent accent a pretty green and white cottage at 49 Embury Avenue.

A wondrous display of cutout work adorns the front of 70 Pilgrim Pathway, while trees confound the photographer!

Brick red and off white add accent to a towering sky blue edifice on the corner of Webb and Pennsylvania Avenues.

Wooden lace was lavished on this home at 84 Webb Avenue, and lovingly presented with appropriately feminine strokes of pink and white.

Pretty applied woodwork was used to create a sunburst and decorative cornices on this home at 75 Webb Avenue.

Pretty colors dress up a nicely trimmed home at 69 Webb Avenue.

Sea Angel's Dream was the fantasy of Carolyn and John Eckels before they retired here. They have lovingly restored and landscaped this circa 1873 home at 73 Webb Street.

A loving hand has applied decorative detail above and beyond what bric-a-brac woodwork the carpenter left behind on this Webb Avenue home.

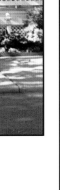

White gingerbread detail adorns a baby blue home at 57 Webb Avenue.

Bright yellow broadcasts good cheer from this circa 1879 structure at 51 Webb Avenue.

Somewhat of an anomaly in this town, the Middle Eastern motifs are certainly in keeping with Victorian times. A passion for exploration in "colonized" countries around the globe fed an interest in both the United States and England for all things exotic.

Purple and green help highlight the wonderful window mouldings at 31 Webb Avenue.

A picket fence demonstrates the difficulty of maintaining wood at the shore, where it must be carefully protected by paint.

Pretty houses, all in a row, stretching east along Webb Avenue.

This pretty gingerbread on Webb Avenue is dated 1890.

Gail Schaffer has lived at 7 Embury Avenue for over forty years, slowly and lovingly restoring it. Her pride and joy are the twenty-five-paned stained glass panels that top the sliders in all of the windows that front her home. She lights them up at night, providing a free show for all. The Victoria, as its dubbed, has "1897" scrawled in the attic, so she assumes that this home was built the same year that Queen Victoria celebrated her diamond jubilee.

A detail shot highlights pretty purple and pink interplay at Mt. Hermon Way and Whitefield Avenue.

A circular window with spokes is an unusual adornment in this town, here topping 132 Mt. Tabor Way.

It is impossible for new homes today to enjoy balustrades like this one on Mt. Tabor Way. Safety codes prohibit the creation of woodwork that children can climb, and then tumble over. Everyone benefits in that the fact that these have been preserved.

Waves of colorful shingles ascend the central column of a large, lakefront home at the terminus of Benson and Lake avenues.

A small cottage, circa 1874, at 61 Delaware Avenue.

Scalloped vergeboard provides a modicum of dress to 140 Mt. Hermon Way.

Cupid caps this asymmetrical cottage at 65 Delaware Avenue.

A loving hand has retouched the intricate detailing found at 69 Delaware Avenue, where carved appliqué adds another layer to moulding, turned posts, and gingerbread detailing.

A cottage is all but hidden by the expanses of gingerbread work wrapping it at 77 Delaware Avenue.

The timbers supporting the roof at 9 Pilgrim Pathway were dressed in lovely cutwork, and are still lovingly painted today. The pent roof helps to keep the porch cool.

A small cottage serves year round as home to many in Ocean Grove. These petite treasures stand at 106 and 106-1/2 Cookman Avenue.

A patriotic theme characterizes this home on the corners of Cookman and New Jersey avenues.

A red and yellow cottage at 64 Clark Avenue was wrapped in gingerbread, and made to appear larger in contrast to a "whale."

118

Pretty vergeboard and appliqués over the second-floor windows characterize this house at 100 Webb Avenue.

A darker palette succeeds in focusing the eye on the front porch at 84 Main Avenue.

A colorful little cottage, set off with a hedge at 88 Main Avenue.

Moulding over the first-floor windows add architectural interest to 86 Main Avenue.

An interesting portico provides a focal point at 104 Main Avenue.

A great, blue tower with a conical roof and a flared chimney are eyecatchers at 108 Main Avenue.

Pretty details add welcome to the porch at 112 Main Avenue.

Carefully restored, Nagles still offers a museum like display of, the pharmacy of yesterday, but the only prescription they offer customers today is the healing influence of ice cream following a selection from a long list of menu choices.

Layers of detail have been added to this cottage, a private residence that occupies prime real estate on Main Avenue.

The Eagle Hook and Ladder – Station #2 is one of three volunteer fire companies in Ocean Grove.

A little cottage on Abbott Avenue.

The original Neptune High School was built in 1898, and designed by architects Brouse & Arend. It is a fine example of adaptive reuse by a group of Ocean Grove volunteers who helped turn the building into the Jersey Shore Arts Center with a beautifully restored 600-seat auditorium.

A blue cottage, complete with three-storey tower, at 75 Abbott Avenue.

Intricate spindle work fills every nook in post and beam on this cottage at 73 Abbott Avenue. Such woodwork is difficult to maintain under any circumstance, most especially so in the harsh climate of salt air.

Ocean Grove Gourmet, one of the special shops in Ocean Grove.

This massive three story cedar shake tower stands sentinel at 122 Pilgrim Pathway.

A beautiful site, 107 Mt. Hermon Way stands across from a park dedicated to local firemen and other Ocean Grove leaders.

MORE SCHIFFER TITLES

www.schifferbooks.com

Cape May's Gingerbread Gems. Tina Skinner & Bruce Waters . Sixty-five color images of summer cottages and guesthouses create a treasured souvenir for all who have visited New Jersey's southern cape, and an indispensable reference for anyone who loves Victorian Era architecture and exterior orna-mentation. This is a visual smorgasbord  of Victorian architecture and ornamentation, adorned with sparkling coats of colorful paint. Gorgeous examples of Carpenter Gothic, Gothic Revival, Italianate, Second Empire, Edwardian, American Bracketed Villa, and Stick Styles are presented. Most date from the late 1800s to the early 1900s, and all are dripping with finely wrought wood bric-a-brac and ornaments. Includes work by celebrated architects Frank Furness, Samuel Sloan, and Stephen Decatur Button. This selection of summer cottages and guesthouses was drawn from one of the greatest collections of late 19th century buildings in the United States.

Size: 5 7/8" x 5 7/8"   65 color photos   64 pp.
ISBN: 0-7643-2126-9   hard cover $9.95

Gingerbread Gems: Victorian Architecture of Cape May. Tina Skinner & Bruce Waters. Cape May has a visual smorgasbord of Victorian architecture and ornamentation, adorned with sparkling coats of colorful paint. Gorgeous examples of Carpenter Gothic, Gothic Revival, Italianate, Second Empire, Edwardian, American Bracketed Villa, and Stick Styles are pre-sented in color, most dating from the late 1800s to the early 1900s, and all dripping with finely  cut wood bric-a-brac. Work by celebrated national architects Samuel Sloan and Frank Furness is featured, along with the area's premier local designer, Stephen Decatur Button. This pic-ture-packed volume of summer cottages and guesthouses is a treasured souvenir for all who have visited New Jersey's south-ern cape, and an indispensable reference for enthusiasts of Vic-torian era architecture and exterior ornamentation.

Size: 8 1/2" x 11"   150 color photos   80 pp.
ISBN: 0-7643-1971-X   soft cover $19.95

Doorways of Cape May. Tina Skinner & Me-lissa Cardona. If eyes are windows to a person's soul, doorways reveal the nature of a place and the people who inhabit it. Wel-come to Cape May, New Jersey, home to the nation's largest concentration of historic Vic-torian architecture! Filled with 65 charming color photos, this book welcomes you to explore some of the most picturesque and historic doorways. They feature wooden

scrollwork and bright coats of paint, as well as Cape May's no-table custom screen doors, advertising to all a pride of owner-ship in front porch appointments. This book is the perfect sou-venir for Cape May visitors, lovers of Victorian architecture, and homeowners looking for distinctive ideas for their front doors.

Size: 6" x 9"   65 color photos   64 pp.
ISBN: 0-7643-2161-7   hard cover $9.95

Cape May Point: Three Walking Tours of His-toric Cottages. Joe Jordan. Whether you are visitor, vacationer, or resident, this tour book will be your indispensable guide to the history and charm of Cape May Point, New Jersey, as you stroll past its wonderful collection of nine-teenth-century cottages. Three walking tours encompass more than 70 of Cape May Point's  earliest buildings - each illustrated in full color with engaging descriptions of their architec-tural features. Each tour is a delightful way to spend a leisurely hour or so. Additionally, two-dozen rare photographs portray handsome houses that did not survive the ravages of develop-ment and storms that devastated one-fifth of the original com-munity. Ten "top pick" contemporary homes are also featured and described. If you cannot tell a baluster from a bargeboard, have no fear. The fully illustrated glossary interprets any pro-fessional jargon so that you will soon become knowledgeable about domestic Victorian architecture. Cape May Point attracts many for its delightful cottages, intimate scale, gracious town plan, and preserved natural beauty. How did this combination happen? And what are the distinctive architectural results? This book will tell you and present the magic of Cape May Point. Read and explore.

Size: 6" x 9"   132 color & b/w photos   144 pp.
ISBN: 0-7643-2108-0   soft cover $14.95

Schiffer books may be ordered from your local bookstore, or they may be ordered directly from the publisher by writing to:
Schiffer Publishing, Ltd.
4880 Lower Valley Rd
Atglen PA 19310
(610) 593-1777; Fax (610) 593-2002
E-mail: Info@schifferbooks.com

Please visit our web site catalog at *www.schifferbooks.com* or write for a free catalog. Please include $3.95 for shipping and handling for the first two books and $1.00 for each additional book. Free shipping for orders $100 or more.

Printed in China

MORE SCHIFFER TITLES

www.schifferbooks.com

Naughty Victorians and Edwardians: Early Images of Bathing Beauties. Mary L. Martin & Tina Skinner. Most are modest, some dare smoke and strike suggestive poses. Others go so far as to expose an inch of flesh as they coyly wring seawater from their swim dresses. Enjoy over 100 hand-tinted postcards taken during an era when women may have been clothed from 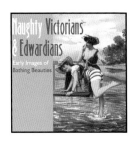 head to toe, but they were women nonetheless. Dressed in the latest beach fashions, bold Victorians flirt with the camera, creating charming and beguiling images..

Size: 6" x 6"   105 color photos   96 pp.
ISBN: 0-7643-2115-3   hard cover $12.95

Cape May Point: The Illustrated History from 1875 to the Present. Joe Jordan. The smallest shore resort on the New Jersey coast, Cape May Point has more than one million visitors each year! This beautiful depicts Cape May Point's wonderful gingerbread cottages, Victorian chapels, and bantam bungalowsthat are turning into plastic palaces. Learn about the grand hotels, the two disastrous fires, President Harrison's 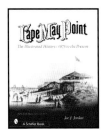 scandal, the religious revivals and camp meetings, the Country Club, and, of course, the devastating storms that affected the Point. Take a nostalgic journey to Cape May Point's immediate neighbors: the old Life Saving Station, Sunset Beach, the New Jersey State Park, the former South Cape May, the Lighthouse, and Higbee's Beach. Illustrated with over 200 classic photos and drawings, this book will delight vacationers and residents,and inspire future generations of shore-goers.

Size: 8 1/2" x 11"   202 b&w photos & illustrations 144 pp.
ISBN: 0-7643-1830-6   hard cover $24.95

Lighthouse Views: North America's Best Beacons Captured on Postcards. Tina SkinnerMary Martin Postcards. Just as the Victorians once traveled the shorelines in search of scenic lighthouses, collecting postcards to document their discoveries, people today react to the allure of these lights that draw tourists, collectors, and maritime fans. This book examines the postcard keepsakes that lighthouse lovers have collected since the 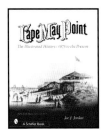 turn of the 20th Century, documenting lighthouses from California to Alaska, and the Florida Keys to Nova Scotia. You'll see lighthouses from land, air, and sea levels in hand-tinted photographs and line drawings produced at the turn of the century, beautiful linen prints of the 1930s and '40s, and contemporary photochrome

productions. Along with the images, lighthouse history and facts are conveyed, along with publishing information to help collectors identify and date their own cards. Values are shown in the captions.

Size: 8-1/2" x 11"   400 color photos   128 pp.
ISBN: 0-7643-2087-4   soft cover $24.95

Cape May Postcards. Victorian architecture, quaint streets, and beautiful beaches have made Cape May, New Jersey, a top tourist attraction for over a century. Forty full-color postcards capture the charm and essence of this picturesque town. Keep it as a souvenir  book, detach and mail the postcards, or show them off in standard 5" x 7" frames. At forty cents per card, you won't find a better deal.

Size: 5" x 7 1/4"   40 color postcards   40 pp.
ISBN: 0-7643-2305-9   soft cover $14.95

Touring New Jersey's Lighthouses. Mary Beth Temple and Patricia Wylupek . New Jersey's coastal heritage is a proud one, with lighthouses playing a starring role. This book visits eleven lighthouses accessible to the public, exploring their history as proud community sentinels and guardians of sea traffic passing treacherous rocks and shoals. From the Sandy Hook lighthouse in the north — the nation's oldest beacon — to popular tourist destination Cape May 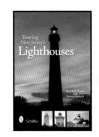 Point on the southern tip of the state, you can explore a great variety of styles, including the fortress-style Twin Lights, Victorian Gothic, and iron towers thrust into the sky. This is the perfect introductory tour, with a general history of lighthouses, and a thoroughly researched overview of the each light's history and function. If you have already visited some or these lights, this book will serve as a great memento. If you' have yet to discover these proud sentinels, this book will help you plan an adventure.

Size: 6x9   67 color photos   96 pp.
ISBN: 0-7643-2093-9   soft cover $9.95

Schiffer books may be ordered from your local bookstore, or they may be ordered directly from the publisher by writing to:
Schiffer Publishing, Ltd.
4880 Lower Valley Rd
Atglen PA 19310
(610) 593-1777; Fax (610) 593-2002
E-mail: Info@schifferbooks.com

Please visit our web site catalog at *www.schifferbooks.com* or write for a free catalog. Please include $3.95 for shipping and handling for the first two books and $1.00 for each additional book. Free shipping for orders $100 or more.

Printed in China

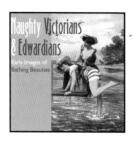

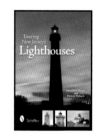